Protists

Algae, Amoebas, Plankton,
and Other Protists

By
Rona Arato

Crabtree Publishing Company
www.crabtreebooks.com

Crabtree Publishing Company

www.crabtreebooks.com

Author: Rona Arato
Series consultant: Sally Morgan, MA, MSc, MIBiol
Project director: Ruth Owen
Designer: Alix Wood
Editors: Mark Sachner, Adrianna Morganelli
Proofreader: Molly Aloian
Project manager: Kathy Middleton
Production coordinator: Katherine Berti
Prepress technician: Katherine Berti

Developed & Created by Ruby Tuesday Books Ltd

Front cover: Colored scanning electron micrograph (SEM) of diatoms. These single-celled algae form an important part of the plankton at the base of the marine and freshwater food chains.

Title page: Brown and green seaweeds

Photographs:
Alamy: page 25
FLPA: pages 4 (main), 7, 10–11 (main), 22 (top), 23 (top), 24, 34, 35, 39
Science Photo Library: front cover, pages 4 (top), 6, 9, 11 (inset), 13, 14–15 (main), 15 (inset), 17 (top), 18 (top), 18 (bottom), 19, 20, 21, 23 (bottom), 26, 27, 28 (top), 28 (bottom), 29, 30, 31 (main), 33, 36, 37, 38, 40–41
Shutterstock: pages 1, 16 (all), 17 (main), 22 (bottom), 31 (top), 32
Wikipedia: pages 42 (top), 42 (bottom), 43

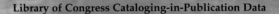

Library and Archives Canada Cataloguing in Publication

Arato, Rona
        Protists : algae, amoebas, plankton, and other protists / Rona Arato.

(A class of their own)
Includes index.
ISBN 978-0-7787-5377-3 (bound).--ISBN 978-0-7787-5391-9 (pbk.)

1. Protista--Classification--Juvenile literature.
2. Protista--Juvenile literature. I. Title.
II. Series: Class of their own

QR74.5.A73 2010   j579.01'2   C2009-907488-5

Library of Congress Cataloging-in-Publication Data

Available at Library of Congress

Crabtree Publishing Company

www.crabtreebooks.com   1-800-387-7650

Printed in the U.S.A./012010/BG20091216

Published in Canada
Crabtree Publishing
616 Welland Ave.
St. Catharines, Ontario
L2M 5V6

Published in the United States
Crabtree Publishing
PMB 59051
350 Fifth Avenue, 59th Floor
New York, New York 10118

Published in the United Kingdom
Crabtree Publishing
Maritime House
Basin Road North, Hove
BN41 1WR

Published in Australia
Crabtree Publishing
386 Mt. Alexander Rd.
Ascot Vale (Melbourne)
VIC 3032

Contents

Introduction **What Are Protists?** 4

Chapter 1 **The Biology of Protists** 12

Chapter 2 **Algae: The Plant-Like Protists** 20

Chapter 3 **Protozoa: The Animal-Like Protists** 29

Chapter 4 **Slime Molds and Other Fungus-Like Protists** 36

Glossary 44

Further Information 46

Index 47

About the Author 48

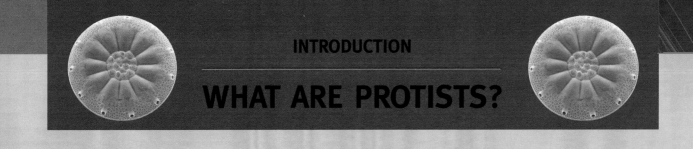

WHAT ARE PROTISTS?

Even if you've never tasted a piece of seaweed, you probably eat foods, such as ice cream, that are made with some type of protist. The water you drink is purified by bacteria-eating protists. Protists are in many household products, as well. When you use shampoo, for example, protists make your hair shine!

A Diverse Group

Protists come in hundreds of shapes, sizes, and forms. Some live alone, others in giant colonies. They float, swim, creep, and crawl. Many protists are invisible to the naked eye, and there are others, such as giant kelp and other seaweeds, that can be seen clearly without a microscope.

CASE STUDY

Kingdom or Domain?

EUKARYA

Protists
Plants
Animals
Fungi

BACTERIA

ARCHAEA

The way life-forms are grouped, or classified, is constantly changing. Traditionally, organisms were classified as either animal or plant. Over the years, many organisms have been grouped *alongside* animals and plants, rather than *within* those two groups. For years, the classification of living things has been based on six *kingdoms* of life—animals, plants, fungi, protists, bacteria, and archaea.

As scientists improve their understanding of the genetic makeup of living things, they can better compare organisms. This understanding has helped scientists figure out even more detailed groupings of living things. In the past, organisms were grouped according to their appearance. Appearances can be misleading, however. Two organisms may look similar, but their genetic makeup can be very different. For example, some yeasts might look like bacteria based on the fact that, like bacteria, they consist of a single round cell. Today, yeasts are known to be fungi, not bacteria.

Most scientists now believe that organisms should be classified using an even bigger grouping than kingdom. This level is called the *domain*. These scientists propose that life should be divided into three domains—Eukarya, Bacteria, and Archaea. Within the domain Eukarya are the four kingdoms of animals, plants, fungi, and protists. These kingdoms are more closely related to each other than to the domains of bacteria and archaea.

This is where things stand—for now. As scientists continue to make new discoveries, this system will undoubtedly turn out to be another chapter in the story of life!

We probably give little thought to these large organisms other than that they seem like somewhat exotic forms of plant life. If this is the impression you have had of larger protists, then you may be forgiven for being wrong— just as scientists were also wrong for centuries in their view that some protists were plants and others animals!

A Kingdom of Their Own

Protists are a group of organisms that were first identified in 1674. That was the year that Anton van Leeuwenhoek, a Dutch scientist, looked at a drop of water through a microscope and saw hundreds of tiny creatures swimming around.

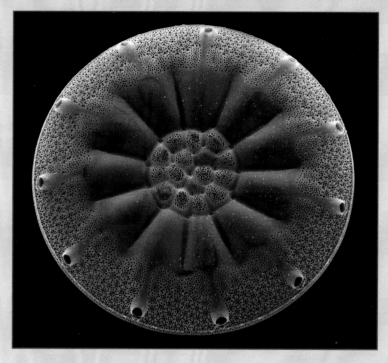

Tiny single-cell diatoms—a type of algae—have an amazing appearance when viewed with a powerful scanning electron microscope (SEM).

One type of protist, the giant kelp, grows in "forests" in shallow ocean waters. Sea otters tether themselves to the kelp's long, wavy strands to keep them from floating out to sea while they sleep.

Van Leeuwenhoek called the organisms he saw through his microscope "animalcules," which means "little animals," because that's what he thought they were. After studying them more thoroughly in the centuries that followed van Leeuwenhoek's discovery, researchers realized that they were neither animals nor plants.

Over time, scientists classified protists as a separate kingdom. It is called Protista, which means "the very first." Although it is not likely that all protists were among the first life-forms, there are fossils of some species that date back several billion years ago, making them among the oldest-known organisms to appear on the planet. Today, scientists estimate that over 200,000 types, or species, of protists exist.

So What Is a Protist?

One way of defining protists is to explain what they are *not*. They are not plants, animals, bacteria, or fungi. Like plants, animals, and fungi, protists are *eukaryotic*. This means that their cells have a nucleus—the part of a living cell that controls its growth and its genetic characteristics—that is wrapped in a membrane. They are thus more complex than bacteria, which are *prokaryotic*. This means that bacteria do not have a nucleus wrapped in a membrane.

WHY DO WE CALL THEM EUKARYOTES?

The word eukaryotes comes from the Greek word meaning "seed." This is because the nucleus contains a cell's genes—the material that carries an organism's characteristics and passes them on to the next generation. Animal, plant, fungi, and protist cells have nuclei. Bacteria have genetic material, but it is not contained in a membrane envelope. Scientists have named bacteria prokaryotes, which means "before eukaryotes."

FEEDING THEMSELVES AND OTHERS

Some protists are autotrophic. This means that, like plants, they make their own food using sources of energy found in nature, such as sunlight. The protists Euglena gracilis (shown here) are photosynthetic—they synthesize food using the Sun's energy in the same way as plants. Others are heterotrophic, like animals, and eat other organisms. Protists also provide food for other life-forms. They make up large portions of the plankton that is an important ecosystem sustaining much of the life, such as fish and shellfish, in Earth's oceans.

A THING FOR WET PLACES

Most protists are unicellular and are invisible to the naked eye. That means you can only see them with a microscope. Others are multi-cellular or colonial and are clearly visible. Although protists are a varied group, with many differences in size and shape, they do share certain characteristics. They usually live in wet places, such as oceans, lakes, damp forest floors, in the water that flows into your kitchen sink, and in the intestines of animals, humans included. Here, a diver swims above a colony of freshwater algae.

As we have seen, protists come in many shapes and sizes. Some, such as amoebas, are single-celled organisms that can only be seen though a microscope. Others, like kelp, are made up of many cells that are grouped together and look like huge plants.

These protists, which can grow in strands up to 30 feet (100 meters) long, are multi-cellular and are thus more complex than single-celled bacteria. They are less complex than most plants, animals, or fungi, however, because they do not have specialized organs, such as leaves, roots, or stems, that have jobs to perform.

In plants, animals, and fungi, each specialized organ is made up of different types of cells. Multi-cellular protists, such as kelp and other seaweeds, are made up of numerous cells, but they are mainly the same kind and do not develop into specialized organs.

Some protists are colonial, which means that they live in large groups and are also clearly visible. What you see in these cases are many protists, such as algae and slime mold, clumped together. Like other protists that are multicellular, the uniformity of their cell structure makes colonial protists relatively simple compared to most plants, animals, and fungi.

The Classification of Organisms

Scientists have already identified about two million species of organisms, and they think there are millions more waiting to be discovered. In order to study them, scientists have organized these species into groups with similar characteristics. This process is called *classification*. When classifying a species, scientists look at the history of how that species evolved. Organisms that developed along similar evolutionary patterns, or those that share similarities in shape or size, may be classified close together.

Scientists now know that even though two organisms may look alike, they can be very different in their makeup. Every organism has its own genetic characteristics.

In more recent years, the classification of one organism in relation to another may depend less on their appearance and more on their DNA—the material that carries the genetic codes handed down from one generation of an organism to another. In this book, we will look at protists less from the standpoint of their genetic makeup and more along the lines of size, shape, appearance, and behavior that have typically caused them to be classified as they are.

No matter what criteria are used to classify organisms, there are eight major levels that are usually used to group protists and other life forms: domain, kingdom, phylum (or *division* in plants), class, order, family, genus, and species. To understand it, let's look at the way scientists classify a single species of amoeba, called *Amoeba proteus*, or *A. proteus* for short.

CLASSIFICATION OF AN AMOEBA

Domain:	Eukarya
Kingdom:	Protista
Phylum:	Protozoa
Class:	Sarcodina
Order:	Amoebida
Family:	Amoebidae
Genus:	*Amoeba*
Species:	*Amoeba proteus*

A light micrograph of the single-celled protozoan Amoeba proteus

This protozoan has blunt protuberances around it known as pseudopodia, or "false feet." The protozoan uses the pseudopodia to move. It extends a pseudopodium in the direction it wants to go, anchors it, and the cytoplasm from the rest of the cell flows forward into the pseudopodium.

The body of the cell consists of a mass of cytoplasm with a nucleus.

Why Are Protists Important?

Many protists are invisible to the naked eye. Some species cause terrible diseases. When lumped together with similar protists, some look like the kinds of slimy messes your mother would scream at you for bringing into the house on the bottom of your shoes! So why do scientists study them? Why are they an important part of our world?

It's hard to know how many individual organisms there are of any group on the planet, but scientists estimate that trillions of individual protist organisms are probably alive at any given moment. Many are important sources of food, for humans and for other animals. Some form part of the plankton that floats on or near the surface of ocean waters. Many of the organisms making up the plankton are photosynthesizing. That is, like plants, they use

Gills

energy from the Sun to make food. Other water-dwelling animals, such as whales, fish, and seals, benefit when they feed on the plankton. Even more important—and also like plants—protists take from the atmosphere the carbon dioxide that most animals do not need and release the oxygen that animals need to survive.

It's true that some protists cause dreadful human diseases such as malaria, dysentery, and African sleeping sickness, and others, such as the dinoflagellates that cause the "red tide," kill sea life. Most protists are harmless, however, and many, such as the paramecia that eat harmful bacteria, are very helpful. Protists are used in food, cosmetics, and medicine. They are also invaluable in research, as scientists study them to learn more about Earth's ecosystems and human disease.

Growing to an average length of 26 feet (eight meters), basking sharks may be huge, but they survive by eating microscopic plankton—millions of them every hour! They filter the plankton from the water through their gills using brush-like gill rakers.

A "red tide" caused by algae off the coast of Australia

CHAPTER ONE

THE BIOLOGY OF PROTISTS

With over 200,000 species estimated on our planet, protists are a very diverse group, with many differences among them. They do share some common features, however.

One Kingdom with Plenty of Diversity

As we have seen, protists range in size from the tiniest microscopic specs to giant kelp that can grow up to 100 feet (30 m) long. The cells of some protists, such as algae, have highly specialized chloroplasts, in which photosynthesis takes place, allowing them to use energy from the Sun to produce nutrition out of carbon dioxide and water. This is one way in which these protists resemble plant cells. Others, such as paramecia, move around a great deal and resemble animals. Another group, the sporozoans, don't move at all.

The Cell Structure of a Protist

As we have also seen, protists also share certain important characteristics. As eukaryotes (pronounced "you-carry-oats"), protists have cells that contain a nucleus that is separated from the rest of the cell by a thin membrane.

Protists have a simple cellular structure compared to more specialized cells in plants, animals, and fungi. They are much more complex than the single-celled bacteria, however, which are made up of cytoplasm inside a cell membrane. The cell membrane is surrounded by a cell wall. Bacteria have parts within their cytoplasm, but they have no nuclei or other parts bound by membranes. In contrast, protists have many parts, but the fact that the nucleus is encased in a membrane sets it apart from the rest of the cell and makes it more specialized and thus very important. The nucleus contains most of the cell's genetic material.

Outside of the nucleus is the cell's cytoplasm. This is the substance that contains both the nucleus and other parts of the cell.

Other tiny particles inside the cell are called organelles. Organelles are highly specialized structures with specific jobs to do. These parts include mitochondria, which take in oxygen, and plastids, which use sunlight to produce energy. Chloroplasts, mentioned earlier, are also organelles.

Some protists have food vacuoles—membrane-bound vesicles containing water and food particles. The organism pours digestive enzymes into the food vacuole. This enables the organism to digest the food and absorb the soluble products.

The Parts of a Protist Cell

An illustration of a Euglena gracilis *protist*

Flagellum

Mitochondria—the organelles that generate energy in a cell. They lie in the cytoplasm of the cell.

Nucleus

Cytoplasm

Contractile vacuole—an organelle that forces water out of the cell. This reduces pressure inside the cell and keeps it from bursting.

Chloroplasts—specific types of plastids that are found in the cells of green plants and in photosynthetic algae, where photosynthesis takes place

Plastids are the organelles in a cell, such as a chloroplast, that synthesize and store food and/or pigments.

Photosynthetic Protists

When humans prepare a meal, we make it out of existing foods or products that can be processed or prepared to create the meal. These include fruits, vegetables, meats, oils, grains, or dairy products. When a photosynthetic plant or protist makes a meal, it creates its food from scratch. This means that it carries out a process called photosynthesis. In this process, the organism takes in carbon dioxide—a gas that the organism requires—and releases back into the environment oxygen—a gas that humans must breathe. Life as we know it could not exist without plants and photosynthetic protists.

Photosynthetic protists use light, carbon dioxide, and water to create their own nutrients, just like plants do. These protists include algae, dinoflagellates, and euglena.

Amoeba

Pseudopodium

Paramecium

Heterotrophic protists

Not all protists use photosynthesis to create their food. Many protists are heterotrophic. This means that they eat "ready-made" organic material. It also means that they must find this food and then ingest it. Protists do this in many ways. An amoeba creeps toward its prey and then surrounds and traps it with projections of its surface, called pseudopodia, that it extends for the purpose of getting around and catching food. Some protists, such as protozoa, are ciliates. This means that they have rows of structures called cilia, which are very fine, hair-like projections that help the organism move and catch its food. Cilia help protozoa eat by sweeping up juicy morsels for the protozoan's meal.

How Do Protists Get Around?

Protists move in many ways. An amoeba may use its pseudopodia, or "false feet," to creep along the bottom of a body of water. Some protists, and other organisms, have slender, whip-like appendages known as flagella which help them move around.

Unlike the ciliates, sporozoans do not have cilia nor flagella and they cannot move at all. They are literally stuck in one place. Sporozoans are thus parasites that live on, or in, the bodies of other organisms. These parasites cause malaria and other diseases in humans.

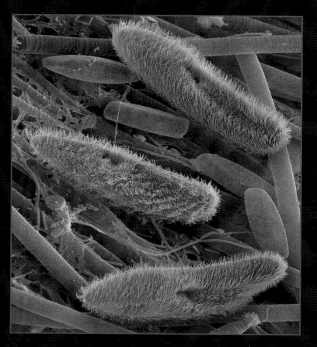

An amoeba engulfs a paramecium. The amoeba has extended a pseudopodium to surround its prey. The paramecium will be digested within the amoeba's food vacuole.

These freshwater aquatic paramecia are covered with cilia (short, hair-like structures), which they use for swimming and sweeping food into their mouths.

What Protists Do For Us

Why do humans need protists? As it turns out, they do quite a lot for us. Without them, many ecological systems and food webs would break down. Protists such as algae make up part of the plankton that lives in watery environments. There, protists and other microscopic organisms provide food for all kinds of animals such as oysters, mussels, and sea urchins. These, in turn, become food for other animals such as fish and sea otters, which are then eaten by larger animals such as whales, seals, and even bald eagles. Many of the animals within this food web are eventually eaten by humans, who then indirectly benefit from the protists, as well.

Marine Food Web

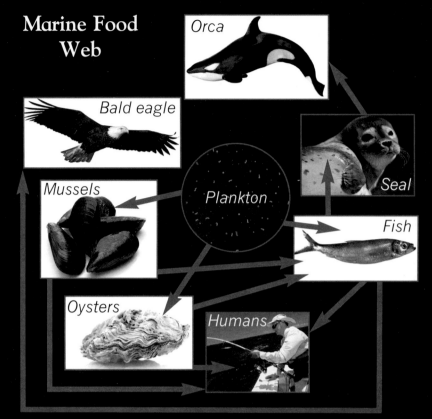

Plankton form the base of this marine food web. The arrows mean "gives food to."

Coccolithophores: Protists on Your Chalkboard

CASE STUDY

You can thank tiny, prehistoric protists for the chalk you use in school. These protists, coccolithophores, helped form the thick chalk beds found in many parts of the world.

Chalk is limestone, a form of calcium carbonate. It is the same substance that makes up seashells and the shells of coccolithophores—tiny protists that live in the ocean. The word coccolith comes from the Greek words that mean "berry" and "stone." Coccolithophores are also known as "chalk makers" because it is the remains of their shells (called coccoliths) that form the chalk beds, such as those that make up the famous White Cliffs of Dover in England. Chalk beds were formed over 65 million years ago in the Cretaceous Period, during the time of the dinosaurs, and they are found all over the world.

The chalk from these long-gone coccolithophores is so prevalent that scientists named the entire era after it. The word cretaceous comes from the Latin creta, which means "chalk." As billions of coccolithophores died, their shells sank to the ocean floor. Over time, they formed layers of calcium carbonate that became the chalk beds. If you look at chalk dust under an electron microscope, you might just see the fossils of tiny coccolithophores.

So remember, when you write on a chalkboard, you are writing with the remains of millions and millions of tiny protists that filled the oceans way back in the age of the dinosaurs.

This picture is a colored scanning electron micrograph (SEM) of small marine protists called coccolithophores. The organisms are covered in coccoliths, which are individual plates of calcite crystals.

The White Cliffs of Dover in England

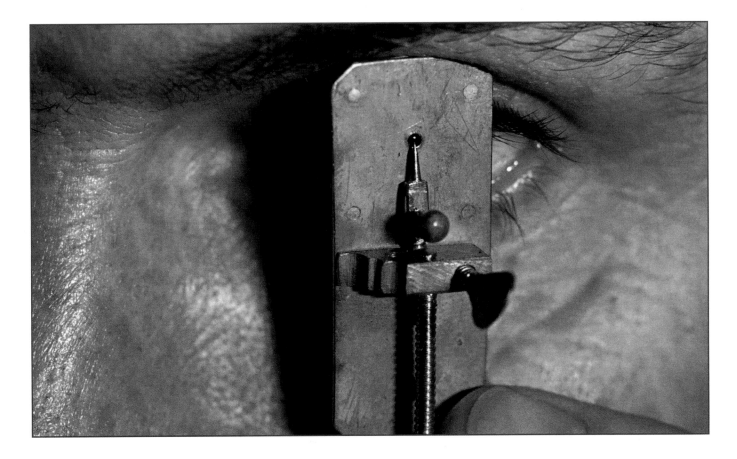

A man looks through the tiny lens of an early microscope made by the Dutch scientist Anton van Leeuwenhoek. The microscope allowed magnifications of up to 200 times.

fig: A *fig:* B C D

fig: E *fig:* G.

fig: F

These are drawings made by Anton van Leeuwenhoek of animalcules he observed when he examined "white matter" from between his teeth and rain water under a microscope.

How Do Protists Reproduce?

Most protists reproduce asexually. Like bacteria and other single-celled organisms that reproduce asexually, they simply split in half. The new cell is an exact copy of the original. Some protists reproduce sexually, and others have life cycles in which they alternate between sexual and asexual reproduction. This pattern is very complex, and it may be more common among certain parasites, which may use the host organism to aid in its own process of reproduction.

These euplotes protozoa are in the final stages of cell division. This single-celled protist reproduces asexually to produce a duplicate of itself.

Animal? Plant? Neither?

The Greek philosopher Aristotle, who lived between 384 and 322 BCE, divided all life into two categories—plants and animals. For 2,000 years, scientists agreed with him. In 1674 Dutch scientist Anton van Leeuwenhoek looked through his homemade microscope and saw a bunch of tiny organisms squiggling around in a drop of water. He couldn't believe his eyes! He wrote to other scientists about the "animalcules" he thought he had found, and soon, they were building microscopes and studying these organisms, as well. Using a term to describe the incredibly tiny things they saw—microbes—they divided the organisms into two groups. The organisms that they saw swimming were called *protozoa* (from the Greek word for "first animals"). The green, plant-like microbes were called *algae* (from the Latin word for "seaweed").

At this point in the classification of these organisms, they were still divided into two kingdoms: plant and animal. In 1866, Ernst Haeckel, a German biologist, decided that the microbes Leeuwenhoek had discovered were so different from any plants or animals that they must be the ancestors of all of them. Haeckel believed they deserved their own kingdom, which he called Protista, based on words from Greek that mean "very first."

CASE STUDY

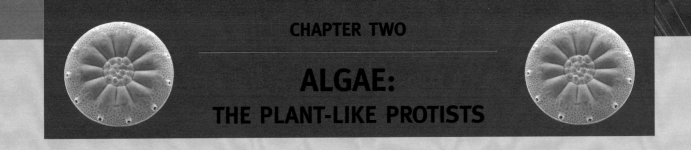

CHAPTER TWO

ALGAE:
THE PLANT-LIKE PROTISTS

Have you ever seen a mass of green scum floating on top of a pond? You may have wrinkled your nose and thought, "Yuck!" Guess what? That scummy stuff is algae, a group of protists with an important job— making oxygen for us to breathe. Scientists believe that algae produce 70–80 percent of the oxygen in our atmosphere.

Why Not a Plant?

Algae look like plants and, like plants, use sunlight to make food from water and carbon dioxide. In return—and also like plants—they release oxygen. This is called photosynthesis. So why aren't they plants?

Unlike plants, which have complex structures, algae are simple. Many are single-celled. Some do have cell walls, but the structure of the cell walls is very different from that of the far more complex plants. Algae are protists, and like other protists, there are only a few environments in which they can live. Most algae are aquatic—they live in water—and a few are terrestrial—they live on land.

This image shows the algae Spirogyra, which forms slimy threads known as "Mermaid's tresses" in stagnant or slow-moving water.

An Ancient Grouping

Today, algae—possibly the first protists to appear on Earth around two billion years ago—come in thousands of species. Unlike most species, which are classified under only one phylum, algae may belong to several different phyla. To simplify the process of grouping them, scientists have divided algae by their colors. These include green algae (phyla Chlorophyta and Gamophyta), yellow-green algae (Xanthophyta), red algae (Rhodophyta), and brown algae (Phaeophyta).

The Colorful World of Algae

In addition to their colors, algae have other features that distinguish them from one another. Brown algae are the largest of all protists. Green algae are the most common. Even these protists come in many shapes and sizes. They range from single cells to large groups of algae that live in colonies. *Acetabularia* is a genus of pinwheel-shaped algae. *Spirogyra* are long, thready algae that are the green "scum" found on ponds.

What Makes Green Algae Green?

No one knows for sure how many species of algae there are today, but there have been estimates placing the number of species of green algae between 6,000 and 7,000. These species are green because they contain a green pigment called chlorophyll. Plants and algae use chlorophyll to convert sunlight into energy. *Chloro* means "green." Chlorophyll is stored within the cell in the organelles called chloroplasts.

ALGAE REPRODUCTION

Spirogyra algae reproduce sexually through a process called conjugation. In spring, threads of the algae come together in pairs. The threads form conjugation tubes. Cytoplasmic mass from the cells of one thread migrate through the tubes and fuse with the cytoplasm in the cells of the second thread. This produces a zygospore (a tough-walled resting structure containing a new cell), which may germinate immediately or lie dormant until the following spring.

Spirogyra *algae threads*

Conjugation tube

Zygospore

Red Algae

Red algae live along the seashore and under the ocean—some as deep as 585 feet (178 m). Red algae look red because they absorb blue light from the water and reflect red wavelengths. Red algae has many uses in addition to being a source of nutrition for sea creatures. Chefs use it to make sushi, and the next time you dig into a bowl of ice cream, remember, red algae is the ingredient that ice cream manufacturers use to make it thick and creamy.

Chondrus crispus *red algae*

Chondrus crispus is a red algae that is bleached in the sun, and then its gelatin is extracted and used for cooking, in textiles, and in cosmetics. It's used in shampoo to give hair a lustrous shine.

Pharmaceutical laboratories use red algae to make agar, a clear, nutrient-rich, gel-like substance. Agar is used in laboratories to grow bacteria for medical research.

Brown and Yellow Seaweeds

Brown algae, also called seaweed, are the largest of all the known protists. These plant-like growths can stretch hundreds of feet. They are found in ocean environments such as the shores of the Atlantic and Pacific oceans on both sides of the United States, on coral reefs in the Caribbean Sea, and on the Great Coral Reef in Australia. They have brown or yellow-brown pigments and can be as small as a single fine strand or as long as 300 feet (91 m).

Seaweed in Our Everyday Lives

Seaweed is a lot more than that annoying stuff that gets wrapped around your feet when you swim in the ocean. Seaweed is used to treat tuberculosis, arthritis, colds, the flu, and worm infections. Seaweed is also becoming more and more popular as a food source, and many people eat it as an alternative to a high-fat meat diet. In Asia, seaweed is considered a delicacy because it is rich in vitamins and minerals. The main types of seaweed are Nori, Kombu, Wakama, and Arame. In fact, it is so popular in Japan, China, and Korea that it is grown in a process called *aquaculture.* This is a low-tech process in which the whole organism is placed in water, where it grows and is tended.

Sheets of Nori, which are used for making sushi

THE ALGAE THAT NAMED A SEA

One type of algae even has a sea named for it. Sargassum is a genus of brown algae with air bladders that keep it afloat on top of the water. The Sargasso Sea in the North Atlantic is named after the masses of sargassum floating on its surface. The Portuguese sailors who first saw it called it "sargaco," which means "grape," because this puffed up seaweed looks like clusters of grapes. Here, sargassum seaweed is growing on the seabed. It will then break off and float on the water's surface.

Below, divers cover an underwater "meadow" of the invasive seaweed Caulerpa with a tarpaulin to stop it from spreading. The seaweed can also be injected with liquid chlorine.

CAULERPA: THE KILLER ALGAE

Caulerpa, a type of seaweed, is perhaps the most common genus of green algae. Caulerpa is a fascinating type of algae, because it is one giant cell that contains multiple nuclei, making it one of the largest cells on Earth. Caulerpa is also fast-growing and invasive. In the Mediterranean Sea and other waters where its growth has gone unchecked, species of Caulerpa have begun crowding out plant life. Once the numbers of plants diminish, fish and other animals that depend on those plants for food will either die out or leave to find food elsewhere, thereby endangering the entire ecological balance of the region.

Dinoflagellates

Dinoflagellates are the whirling dervishes of the protist world. The prefix *dino* means "rotating" or "whirling," which is the way these protists swim. They move by spinning around in the water. They do this with the help of two whipping tails, or flagella. One flagellum stretches behind the protist, while the other flagellum crosses its body, propelling it through the water.

Bioluminescence in Dinoflagellates

Imagine being on a ship in the middle of an ocean at night. You look out and see a bluish glow on top of the water. What is this eerie light, and where does it come from? Long ago, sailors probably thought it was the work of angry gods, but today people know better. The light is called bioluminescence, and it is created by dinoflagellates, one-celled organisms that live in the ocean. Dinoflagellates in an ocean produce light, and it is their glow that can be seen on top of the water.

A dinoflagellate plankton

Flagellum

Dinoflagellates give off their light when they are disturbed, so when a predator comes around, its presence may trigger the light, thereby attracting even larger predators, which will then feed off of whatever it was that was about to eat the dinoflagellates. In this way, bioluminescence is a form of protection.

Bioluminescence is created through a process called oxidation. Certain chemicals interact in the presence of oxygen, resulting in a sparkling light. Since blue wavelengths travel the farthest in water, this is the color that most bioluminescent organisms produce. Those beautiful blue sparks "flying" off the paddle of a boat are really the millions of luminescent dinoflagellates the paddle is pushing around. So pronounced is this effect created by an object moving through water that a satellite can track a submarine by the bioluminescent plankton that "highlights" it as it moves through the water.

The Deadly Red Tide

One of the most spectacular characteristics of dinoflagellates is called a red tide. Red tides are not really tides. They occur when dinoflagellates "bloom," or reproduce in vast numbers and cover the surface of the water, turning it red. These deadly protists release a poison that kills fish and shellfish and can make the people who eat the infected animals sick. If you walk on the beach during a red tide, you might want to hold your nose against the stench of rotting fish!

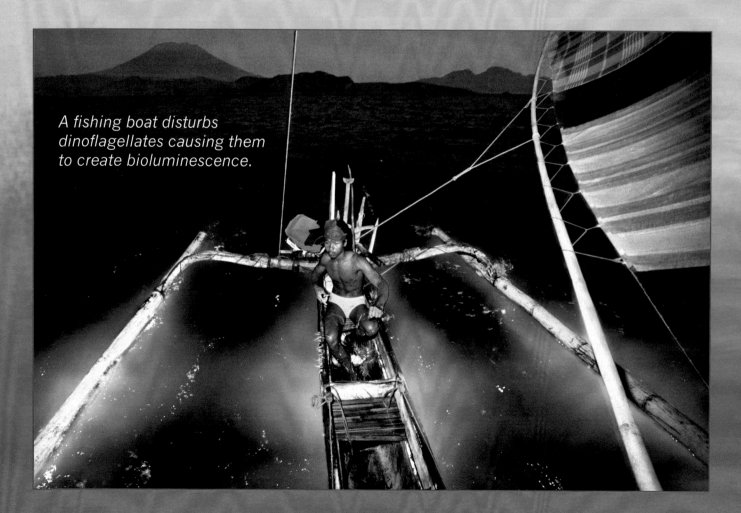

A fishing boat disturbs dinoflagellates causing them to create bioluminescence.

The Beautiful World of Radiolaria and Diatoms

When you walk on a sandy beach, you are walking on the ground-up remains of millions of protists called radiolaria. Radiolaria are single-celled protists with shells of silica, which is a combination of oxygen and silicon. The shells of radiolaria have intricate designs with swirls and spikes. In fact, they are so beautiful that many scientists collect them.

Diatoms are single-shelled protists with sculpted, rounded shells of silica—and what beautiful shells they are! Diatoms are photosynthetic and abundant. They are found in plankton and in sediments in oceans and bodies of freshwater, and they are an important food source for fish and shellfish.

A colored scanning electron micrograph (SEM) of the shell of a radiolarian

The radiolarian moves by projecting its pseudopodia, or "false feet," through these pores in its shell.

Putting Dead Diatoms to Work

Diatoms have been on Earth since the Cretaceous period, for about 140 million years. There are about 10,000 species of diatoms in existence today and about 100,000 extinct species. The extinct diatoms may be gone, but they are not forgotten. As they died, their shells settled onto the bottom of the ancient seas where they lived. Over millions of years, they were packed into the mineral beds and formed a soil-like substance called "diatomaceous earth." You probably aren't aware of it, but you use products with diatomaceous earth every day. Because of its mildly abrasive, porous, and absorptive qualities, diatomaceous earth is used in products such as paint, toothpaste, and swimming pool filters, and to control insects in gardens. When specially processed to be ingested, diatomaceous earth is used to control parasites in animals and humans.

While there are many types of diatoms, they fall into two basic categories: "centric" or round diatoms, and "pennate" or elongated, boat-shaped diatoms. Centric diatoms float in the sea, while the pennate diatoms live on the ocean bottom or on rocks near the seashore.

FROM DIATOM SHELLS TO PLATE GLASS

The silica that makes up diatom shells is an important component of the sand used to make glass. When the sand is melted it becomes transparent and is the basis of the glass used in commercial products.

CASE STUDY

Euglena

Imagine a "plant that can see." Members of the genus *Euglena*–which, like algae, resemble plants– are protists with a dark "eyespot." Scientists think the eyespot is connected to the flagellum and that its purpose is to detect light, prompting the organism to swim toward sunlight, which it needs to conduct photosynthesis and create nutrition.

These organisms live in both fresh and saltwater and have both plant and animal features. They swim and crawl like animals, have chloroplasts and conduct photosynthesis like plants, and, like animals, can even catch and eat tiny bits of food they find in the water. It was this strange creature that helped convince scientists to create the Kingdom Protista nearly 200 years ago.

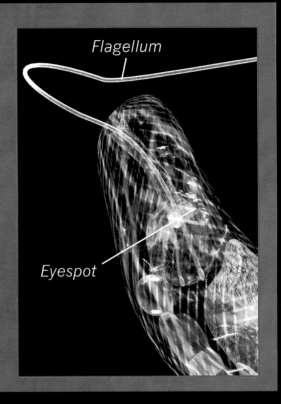

Flagellum

Eyespot

VOLVOX: STRENGTH IN NUMBERS

Volvox is a genus of single-celled protists with double flagella. They live in colonies shaped like hollow spheres on top of the water in deep ponds, lagoons, and ditches. They have red eyespots and chloroplasts, so they make their own food. They are a food source for tiny aquatic creatures, such as rotifers, which are classified as animals but are not much bigger than protists themselves. Volvox reproduce when a small colony breaks away from the mass and forms a new hollow sphere.

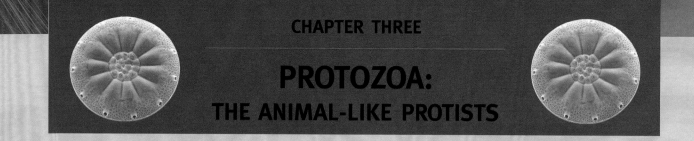

CHAPTER THREE

PROTOZOA:
THE ANIMAL-LIKE PROTISTS

Protozoa are micro-organisms that can look and act like animals but are really protists. They are heterotrophic, which means they eat "ready-made" organic material. Protozoa are found all over the world in freshwater and marine environments, in animal intestines, and sometimes in soil.

How Are They Grouped?

Scientists have classified these interesting organisms into four main groups according to their appearance and how they move: amoebas, ciliates, flagellates, and sporozoans.

Amoebas

These life-forms are fascinating to watch through a microscope as they constantly change shape. In fact, the word *amoeba* comes from a Greek word that means "change." The amoeba's flexible cell membrane moves as the cytoplasm inside pulses against it. This causes the amoeba to form pseudopodia. These "feet" attach to a surface and pull the amoeba along, which is how it moves. When it encounters a tasty morsel, in the shape of an even smaller protist, the pseudopodia wrap around the amoeba's food and completely surround it. The food is trapped in a "food parcel" inside the amoeba, which then digests it by pouring enzymes into the food vacuole and absorbing the products.

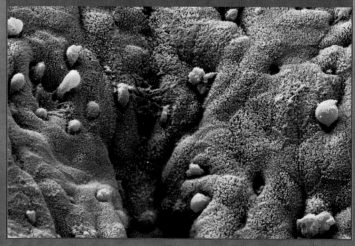

This picture shows colored scanning electron micrograph (SEM) of Entamoeba histolytica *amoebas (blue) invading the lining of the colon.*

AMOEBIC DYSENTERY

Visitors to hot countries such as Mexico sometimes suffer from dysentery, a severe diarrhea that is caused by a parasite that gets into the victim's intestinal tract. Amoebic dysentery is spread through food and water that is contaminated by human feces. Amoebiasis (the medical name for amoebic dysentery) is caused by a protozoa parasite called Entamoeba histolytica. The amoeba can exist for long periods of time in the large bowel (colon). In the vast majority of cases, amoebiasis causes no symptoms. Only ten percent of infected individuals actually become sick.

Amoebas live in watery places such as lakes, rivers, and oceans. They also live in the intestines of animals, including human beings. When the parasitic species *Entamoeba histolytica* gets into human intestines, the result can be severe discomfort and serious diarrhea. This disease is prevalent in areas with a scarcity of clean drinking water. The best way to guard against it is to only drink clean water that has been purified and/or boiled.

Ciliates: Hairy Speed Demons

Ciliates are the speed demons of the protists. There are about 10,000 species of these "hairy" creatures. A single-celled ciliate has dozens, and sometimes hundreds, of tiny hair-like structures that propel this active protist through water. The word *cilia* comes from the Latin word for "eyelash."

Paramecia: The Popular Protozoa

Paramecia (plural for *paramecium*) are among the best known of the ciliates and are fun to watch through a microscope. Their shape, which to some resembles fuzzy bedroom slippers and to others resembles torpedoes, is immediately recognizable. Paramecia live in water, and they move like little boats with dozens of oars that propel them. The "oars" are cilia, which whip back and forth to push the paramecium forward.

The way the cilia work is quite a feat of engineering. The hair-like structures stay stiff as they push ahead through the water. Then, on the backward stroke, they go limp.

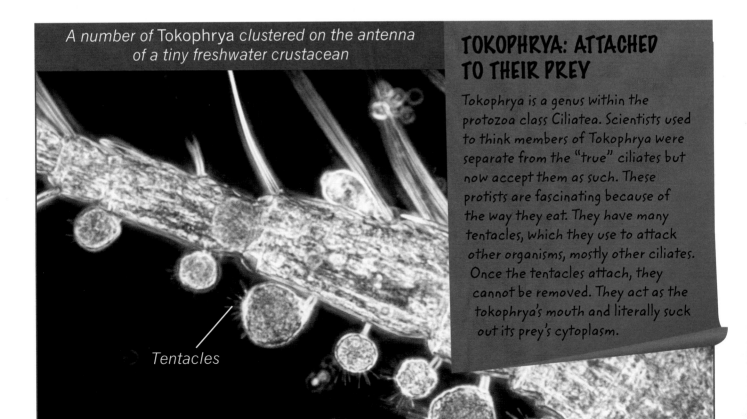

A number of Tokophrya *clustered on the antenna of a tiny freshwater crustacean*

Tentacles

TOKOPHRYA: ATTACHED TO THEIR PREY

Tokophrya is a genus within the protozoa class Ciliatea. Scientists used to think members of Tokophrya were separate from the "true" ciliates but now accept them as such. These protists are fascinating because of the way they eat. They have many tentacles, which they use to attack other organisms, mostly other ciliates. Once the tentacles attach, they cannot be removed. They act as the tokophrya's mouth and literally suck out its prey's cytoplasm.

In this way, the paramecium doesn't slip backward as it zips about. It moves forward until it bumps into another organism or object, and then, instead of turning around, the cilia start moving backward, and so does the paramecium.

Paramecia are not only fun to look at; they are important protists that do a lot of good. Paramecia eat bacteria. Raw sewage is filled with harmful bacteria from human waste. To clean it up, sewage engineers employ these active little protists at sewage plants to gobble up the bacteria so the water that is released into lakes and oceans is clean and safe.

Water treatment pools at a sewage treatment plant

Two slipper-shaped paramecia showing numerous green food vacuoles

Stentor: The Trumpet-Shaped Ciliate

Stentor is a genus of trumpet-shaped unicellular ciliates. They are named after the ancient Greek herald Stentor and his horn. Stentors are among the largest single-celled organisms, occasionally being as much as two millimeters in length. This is still under eight one-hundredths of an inch, but it is long enough to make them just visible to the naked eye and clearly visible with a good magnifying glass. Stentors have a rotating wheel of cilia that create currents in the water. They are found in ponds and lakes, usually near the surface attached to leaves or twigs. Although they can swim on their own, they often cluster together in small colonies.

CASE STUDY

Balantidium coli

Balantidium coli, a ciliate that is known as *B. coli* for short, is the largest protozoa and the only ciliate parasite that infects humans. When it gets into the human intestines, it can cause a disease called balantidiasis that produces symptoms such as diarrhea, abdominal pain, and weight loss. *B. coli* is found all over the world. Pigs carry the parasite, which is often passed to humans when they eat contaminated meat or drink water that has been contaminated with infected feces.

Sporozoans

Sporozoans (the name means "spore producers") are a large group of protozoa that are different from all others because they do not move. They don't have cilia or flagella, and they cannot form pseudopodia. Instead of moving around to find food, they live trapped inside other organisms, where they become parasites. This means they feed off the "host." Sporozoans are not welcome "guests" because they can cause disease and serious illness in their hosts and are easily transmitted from one organism to another.

Two Deadly Diseases Caused by Parasitic Protozoa

Malaria is a terrible disease that, at one time or another, has affected every continent in the world, except Antarctica. Today it is limited mostly to tropical climates. According to the World Health Organization (WHO) 2008 Malaria Report, about 247 million malaria cases were reported in 2006 among 3.3 billion people living in the 109 countries where malaria is widespread. Nearly one million people died, mostly children under five years of age. About 2.5 million children under five years old are infected with malaria each year.

What makes this disease so prevalent and deadly? Malaria is caused by single-celled protozoan belonging to the genus *Plasmodium*. The plasmodia live inside female mosquitoes, where they release a substance that makes the insects so hungry they bite anyone they can find. Every time infected mosquitoes bite someone, they transmit plasmodia into that person's bloodstream. The person's body becomes the ultimate host—a big, wet, warm environment that is the perfect place for plasmodia to reproduce.

Upon entering the host, plasmodia immediately head for the host's liver, where they recreate themselves again and again until there are thousands of these cells swarming through the host's body.

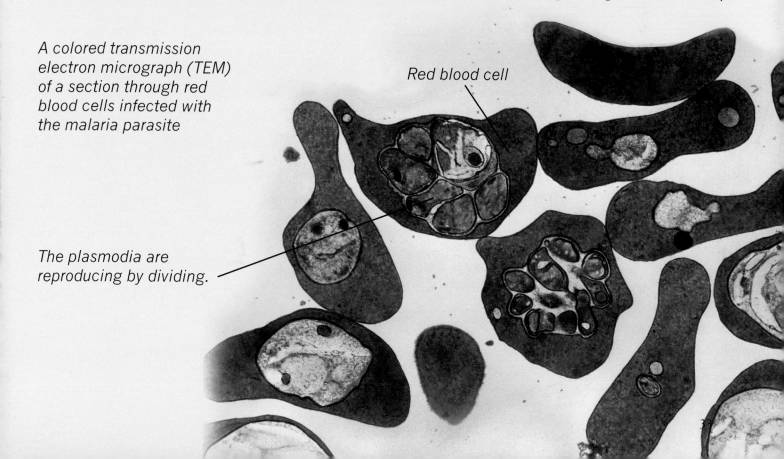

A colored transmission electron micrograph (TEM) of a section through red blood cells infected with the malaria parasite

Red blood cell

The plasmodia are reproducing by dividing.

The invaders activate the host's security system—the white blood cells whose job it is to fend off attackers. Think of the body as a castle. The plasmodia are the invading army and the white blood cells are the defenders. By the time the defenders realize that the castle is under siege, the invaders have swarmed all over it. In a person, this means they have attacked and killed the red blood cells that carry oxygen throughout the body. The host becomes desperately ill and often dies. Those who survive malaria develop serious weakness and usually suffer from malarial attacks for the rest of their lives.

Malaria is spread by mosquitoes that bite infected people and then spread the disease to other people. Although there are treatments, such as quinine, that ease symptoms, the best treatment is prevention.

Today, malaria is most common in hot tropical climates in Africa, South America, Southeast Asia, and parts of China. People living or traveling in these areas are advised to keep their skin covered, especially between sunset and sunrise; use insect repellent on their clothes and any exposed part of their skin; sleep with screens on their windows or under mosquito netting; and, if they have air conditioning, keep it on all day and make sure all windows are closed at night.

African Sleeping Sickness

African Trypanosomiasis is a disease caused by the protozoa species *Trypanosoma brucei*. This organism is a member of a group of protozoa, called trypanosomes, that cause many diseases in humans and livestock. Trypanosomes are related to euglena.

Two adult female mosquitoes feeding on a human

They are long and thin, with a single flagellum. They live and thrive in the human bloodstream, where they swim in a "corkscrew" configuration, twisting around and around as they attack the body's organs. Once a victim is bitten, the parasite reproduces in the bloodstream and lymph nodes. This causes fever, weakness, sweating, pain in joints, and stiffness. Eventually, this deadly parasite gets into the person's brain and causes seizures and then death. Like the mosquito, the tsetse fly transports its deadly passenger from one host to the next, by biting an infected person and then injecting the diseased blood into its next victim.

In spite of modern methods of insect control, the threat of the tsetse fly still hovers over Africa. According to WHO, Human Africa Trypanosomiasis (HAT) and Animal African Trypanosomiasis (AAT), or nagana, occur in 37 sub-Saharan countries covering over 3.5 million square miles (nine million square kilometers). This is about one-third of Africa's total land mass and affects approximately 60 million people. The fly's tiny protist passenger sickens people, horses, and cattle. It has prevented those living in the affected areas from raising livestock and conducting profitable farming. It is estimated that 50,000–70,000 or more people currently suffer from African sleeping sickness and that many millions more have died of the disease. Sleeping sickness is so prevalent that it has held back development in the parts of Africa where the disease is widespread.

The tsetse fly uses its biting mouthparts, which transmit African sleeping sickness.

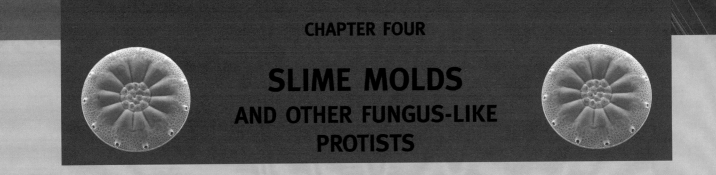

CHAPTER FOUR

SLIME MOLDS
AND OTHER FUNGUS-LIKE PROTISTS

Slime and *mold*. The words alone are probably enough to give most of us a vivid impression of what slime molds must look, feel, and smell like! Yes; some of them do seem disgusting. As with most life-forms, however, our impression of slime molds can change a great deal once we learn more about them.

What Are They?

Slime molds are protists. As we have seen in this book, most protists have characteristics that have led scientists and ordinary people alike to group them at various times with animals, plants, or fungi. Slime molds have characteristics in common with both fungi (such as mushrooms and molds) and other protists (such as amoebas). For years, they were classified as fungi, in part because of their appearance, and also because they are found in places inhabited by fungi, such as on forest floors and in other wooded areas. Also, like some fungi, slime molds live on decaying wood and in most soil, where they feed on bacteria and rotting vegetation.

Slime molds can be red, pink, purple, yellow, white, or orange. They can look like pretzels, nets, berries, puffballs, or slugs.

As with other protists, it's fascinating to compare the different ways in which slime molds "behave" like all the life-forms that they are *not*. As we will see in the brief views of various types, versions, and forms of slime molds that follow, it's no wonder that scientists have had such trouble figuring out just what kind of life form they have been looking at!

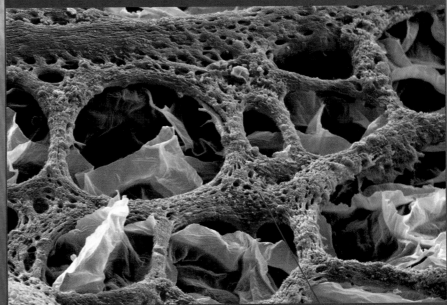

This is a colored scanning electron micrograph (SEM) of slime mold (red) slowly moving and feeding on an almond. The image is magnified 300 times.

The slime is a huge, single cell with multiple nuclei.

SLIME MOLDS: A GREAT RESEARCH TOOL

Biologists like to study slime molds because they are easy to watch as they divide and reproduce. Also, the life cycle of the slime mold is relatively brief. During their short life, these cells move, send out chemical signals, and reproduce in vast numbers. These cycles are similar to those exhibited by cancer cells. Scientists study slime cells to learn about human cell division, especially in cancer cells. Cancer cells have cell cycles that are out of control, which means they keep dividing. Studying rapid cell division in slime molds is helping scientists in their quest to find cures for cancer.

Pretzel slime mold on decaying wood

Plasmodial Slime Molds

Plasmodial slime mold consists of a thin, flat mass of protoplasm. This mass, which is called a plasmodium, doesn't have any cell walls or membranes to break it up into numerous cells, but its protoplasm does contain numerous structures that are similar to cell nuclei. This blob of plasmodium, which may be as long as 12 inches (30.5 centimeters), is often described as one giant cell with thousands of nuclei.

A plasmodium can be red, yellow, or colorless. It looks and feels slimy. It may move along the forest floor in an amoeba-like "creep" and feeds on bacteria, yeasts, and decaying vegetation. This creep is caused by waves of movement within the protoplasm, usually from the back of the plasmodium forward. This movement is usually in response to some kind of outside stimulus, such as the presence of food. Remarkably, this creep, although it is very slow, can often be detected if the observer watches the forward edge of the plasmodium very carefully and patiently.

When a plasmodium is ready to reproduce—usually when its food source is depleted—it creeps over to a place that is dry and sunny, such as the top of a log. Then it settles down and gets to work. The plasmodial slime now reshapes itself into a collection of "fruiting bodies," or sporangia, which appear as a series of thin stalks. Each stalk has a round, bulb-shaped top that looks a bit like a mushroom. This bulb serves as an incubator, protecting the spores or hardened cells that are stored inside. When a wind blows over the bulb, the spores are released into the air, where they float until they are moistened. Then they fall to the ground, re-shape as amoeba, and, once again, make their creepy way across the forest floor to repeat their life cycle.

The slime mold Trichia decipiens

Sporangia (fruiting body)

Spores

Slime mold

CASE STUDY

Fuligo septica: Dog Vomit or Scrambled Eggs?

Fuligo septica is a "shape-shifting" slime mold that goes through a life cycle starting with spores, to yellow slime, to a crusty blob, and then back to spores. It is usually bright yellow but can also be cream, purple, a crusty gray, or powdery brown. In Finland, the slime mold is such a bright yellow that people used to believe that witches used it to spoil milk. It is also called "dog vomit slime mold" or "scrambled-egg slime."

FULIGO SEPTICA

Kingdom:	Protista
Phylum:	Mycetozoa
Class:	Myxomycetes
Order:	Physarales
Family:	Physaraceae
Genus:	Fuligo
Species:	Fuligo septica

Cellular Slime Molds

Cellular slime molds are individually defined cells that resemble amoebas. For most of their lives, these cells creep along by themselves, eating bacteria and decaying vegetation. While they are doing this, they are multiplying asexually. The cells are dividing over and over again, which increases their numbers but also results in their using up the food supply.

At this point, they release a chemical "signal" calling for all the amoebic cells in the area to gather together—which they do, by crawling on top of each other into a mound-shaped mass that moves as a single organism called a pseudoplasmodium. This new organism acts like a plasmodium slime mold, creeping along and gorging on all the bacteria it can find. Eventually, this slug-like creature settles on a log or other sunny location, begins sending out spores that become single amoebas, and eventually—guess what? When these amoebas run out of food, they send out a chemical signal to their fellow amoebas, and start their journey all over again.

Slime Nets

Imagine thousands of long, narrow cells working together to build elaborate road networks, sort of like a freeway system with interconnecting roads. These criss-cross, like in a net. It is this pattern that gives slime nets their name. Slime nets, or labyrinthulids ("little maze" in Latin), are single-celled protists that group together and create "slime trails." They do this by releasing their gelatinous slime through tiny structures located near the organism's membrane. Once they've secreted this sticky goo, they cover themselves with it. Now they have slime above and beneath themselves, creating a kind of "tunnel" around themselves. These slime trails lubricate their path so they can move.

Slime nets live in the sea. They attach themselves to grass growing in shallow water. Sometimes the net gets so big it kills the grass, along with the shellfish that live within its strands. Even if the slime net is destroyed, some cells usually survive to start a new slime colony.

A colored scanning electron micrograph (SEM) of spore towers of the slime mold Dictyostelium discoideum

Collective body of amoebas

Fruiting body on stalk containing spores

A potato crop affected by potato blight

Water Molds: Fungus-Like Protists

Water molds are fungus-like organisms. These molds and downy mildews are parasites that feed on dead organisms and decomposing vegetation. You can identify a water mold by the fuzzy white threads it spins across the surface of dead organic matter. The difference between water molds and fungi, which also live in moist places, is that the water molds' reproductive cells have flagella, while those of fungi don't.

Water molds are important because they cause many plant and animal diseases. For example, *Phytophthora infestans* causes "late blight of potato," the disease that set off the Irish potato famine that killed 1.5 million people.

Phytophthora infestans: The Irish Potato Blight

CASE STUDY

In 1845, the potato crop in Ireland was hit by a terrible blight. Suddenly, the leaves and tubers of the previously healthy potato plants turned brown, then collapsed, and started to rot and stink. What, the farmers wondered, could be causing this terrible tragedy? The culprit was single-celled organisms called *Phytophthora infestans*. Some scientists prefer to classify it as a fungus. Others classify it as a protist. In Ireland at that time, the farmers and peasants depended on the potato for food. For many, it was their only source of food, so they were already undernourished.

When the crop failed, these peasant farmers were left without an important source of vitamins and minerals. During the six years of the famine, from 1845 to 1852, 1.5 million people starved to death and another one million people left Ireland, mostly for the United States. This was a great migration that robbed Ireland of many of its young people and swelled the populations of cities such as New York, Boston, and Chicago.

Plasmopara viticola:
Downey Mildew on Grapes

Downy mildew on grapes occurs all over the world during humid and rainy conditions. It is caused by *Plasmopara viticola*, a protist that attacks all species of grapes. Infected leaves become covered with white or gray spores and develop yellowish-green and clear lesions on their upper surface. As these lesions expand, the leaves turn brown. Eventually, the leaves wither and die. This leaves the young grapes exposed to the Sun.

Wind, rain, and handling of infected plants spread the disease. To control downy mildew, planters are careful to keep the vineyard free of weeds and keep the vines off the ground, where they pick up the spores.

Shriveled grapes exposed to the Sun (left) and a leaf with lesions (below)

Glossary

asexual reproduction Sexless reproduction without adding the genes of one cell to another cell. Some protists reproduce by dividing in half

autotrophic Characteristic of an organism that obtains its carbohydrate nutrients (sugars and starches) from chemical reactions involving a source of energy in the environment, usually the Sun

carbon dioxide A chemical compound made of two oxygen atoms bonded to a carbon atom

cell The smallest unit of life

cell membrane The structure separating all cells from the environment around them; the cell membrane is formed of lipids and contains proteins that help the cell communicate with the environment and take in or put out various substances

cell wall A tough protective covering around a cell, outside the cell membrane

chlorophyll The green substance in a cell that allows it to convert sunlight to energy

chloroplast The part of a protist or plant cell that holds the chlorophyll

chromosome A structure in an organism that contains DNA and protein; eukaryote chromosomes are string-shaped; prokaryote chromosomes are ring-shaped

classification The method scientists use to name and organize organisms into groups

cytoplasm The material inside a living cell, excluding the nucleus

diarrhea Abnormally frequent and watery bowel movements

diatom One-celled colonial algae having cell walls that contain silica

dinoflagellate A single-celled organism, found in plankton and in freshwater, that has two flagella

DNA Deoxyribonucleic acid, a complex molecule that is the blueprint for life, which contains all the "instructions" for building cells; organisms reproduce by replicating their DNA

enzyme A molecule in an organism that is key to making chemical reactions happen—for example, breaking down of food molecules in digestion

euglena Freshwater protist with a reddish "eyespot" and a single flagellum

eukaryotic Having to do with organisms that have a nucleus and other cell parts separated from the rest of the cell by a membrane; plants, animals, fungi, and protists are eukaryotes

flagellum (plural *flagella*) A long, thin, whip-like structure that projects from some protists and is used for movement

gene A segment of DNA that carries the information for a particular trait or the making of a particular protein

genus A group of closely related species

heterotrophic Characteristic of an organism that obtains its nutrients (sugars and starches) from other organisms, dead or alive

host An organism on or in which a parasite or commensal organism lives

infection The presence of disease-causing organisms

malaria A parasitic disease caused by the protist plasmodia that has killed millions of people over the ages

membrane A thin flexible lining that encloses a cell

mitochondria Organelles inside the cell in which the processes of respiration and energy production occur

molecule A grouping of two or more atoms bonded together; the smallest unit of a chemical compound that can take part in a chemical reaction

nucleus Part of the cell that contains its DNA

nutrients Molecules used by the body for growth, repair, and reproduction

organelle A structure in the cell of a eukaryote that has one or more functions and is usually surrounded by a membrane

organic Relating to or derived from living matter; characteristic of a chemical compound that contains carbon

organism A living being; can refer to an individual or a species

paramecium A freshwater protist with an oval body, numerous cilia, and a long, deep oral groove

parasite An organism that feeds on another organism without killing it, or killing it immediately, although the relationship may harm the host

photosynthesis The process by which an organism forms organic molecules using the energy of light

phylum (plural *phyla*) One of the levels of classification of organisms, which from smallest to largest are species, genus, family, order, class, phylum, kingdom, domain. In plants the phylum is called a division

plankton The small or microscopic organisms drifting and floating in water

prokaryotic Having to do with unicellular organisms whose cells do not have a nucleus or other cell parts that are separated from the rest of the cell by a membrane; bacteria and archaea are prokaryotes

pseudopod Literally, "false foot"; a projection on the surface of an amoeba that is used to move and to engulf food

rhodoplast The organelle in red algae that produces its red color

sexual reproduction Production of offspring in which portions of the genetic material of two individuals are combined to produce offspring that are different from either parent

species A group of individual organisms that have so many of the same genes that they are able to mate and exchange DNA

spore A small, often single-celled, resting stage of many organisms; spores are usually able to survive poor environmental conditions that would kill the adult organism

symptom Evidence of physical disease or disturbance as noticed by the patient

vacuole A chamber inside a protist cell where food is sealed

vitamins Nutrients required in small quantities that are not used as building blocks but rather are involved in chemical reactions

white blood cells Cells of the immune system that are found in the bloodstream and find and destroy bacteria and other foreign cells that might do harm to the body

Further Information

http://science.jrank.org/pages/5544/Protista-Classification.html
This Web site explains the Kingdom Protista and helps make sense of a really complex subject.

www.daviddarling.info/encyclopedia/S/slime_mold.html
This Web site is from the Internet Encyclopedia of Science. It's a great site for information on slime molds as well as dozens of other science topics.

www.janthornhill.com/slime-molds.html
Jan Thornhill loves slime molds for their weird and wacky characteristics. She explains what makes them so unique.

http://science.howstuffworks.com/fungi/slime-mold-info.htm
Everything you wanted to know about slime molds. Use this Web site for other science topics, as well.

www.newscientist.com/
Articles and video clips from *New Scientist* magazine highlight some of the coolest new scientific discoveries.

www.nature.com
The latest scientific research and discoveries from the Web site of *Nature* scientific journal.

www.tolweb.org
If you are looking for information about the most current taxonomy (classification) of animal species, you will find it here at the Tree of Life Web Project.

www.sciencedaily.com/news/
For your daily dose of the latest in scientific discoveries, check out the images, articles, and video clips on the Science Daily site.

Index

A

Acetabularia 21
African sleeping sickness 11, 34, 35
African Trypanosomiasis 34
agar 22
algae 5, 7, 8, 11, 12, 13, 14, 19, 20, 21, 22, 23, 24, 25, 26, 27, 28
    brown algae 21, 22, 23
    colors of algae 21
    green algae 21
    phylum of algae 21
    red algae 21, 22
    yellow-green algae 21, 22
Amoeba proteus 9
amoebas 8, 14, 29, 30, 36
    catching prey 15, 29
    movement 9, 15, 29
amoebiasis 29
Animal African Trypanosomiasis (AAT)
animals 4, 6
aquaculture 22
archaea 4
Aristotle 19
autotrophic protists 6

B

bacteria 4, 6, 8, 11, 12, 19, 22, 31, 36
balantidiasis 32
Balantidium coli 32
bioluminescence 24, 25

C

cancer research 37
Caulerpa seaweed 23
cellular slime molds 40

chalk 16, 17
chlorophyll 21
Chlorophyta (phylum) 21
chloroplasts 12, 13, 21
Chondrus crispus 22
cilia 15, 30, 31, 32
ciliates 15, 29, 30, 31, 32
classes (used in classification) 9
classification 4, 8, 9
coccolithophores 16, 17
coccoliths 17
colonial protists 7, 8, 21, 28
contractile vacuoles 13

D

diatomaceous earth 27
diatoms 5, 26, 27
Dictyostelium discoideum 40, 41
dinoflagellates 11, 14, 24, 25
divisions (in classification) 9
DNA 8
domains (in classification) 4, 9
downy mildew 43
dysentery 11, 29

E

Entamoeba histolytica 29, 30
euglena 14, 34
Euglena (genus) 28
Euglena gracilis 5, 13, 28
Eukarya (domain) 4
eukaryotic organisms 6
Euplotes 19

F

families (in classification) 9
flagella 13, 15, 24, 38
flagellates 29

food vacuoles 12, 15, 29, 31
food webs 16
fruiting bodies 38, 41
Fuligo septica 39
fungi 4, 6, 8, 12, 36, 42

G

Gamophyta (phylum) 21
genus 9
giant kelp 4, 5, 8
glass 27
grapes 43

H

Haeckel, Ernst 19, 20
heterotrophic organisms 6, 15, 29
Human Africa Trypanosomiasis (HAT) 35

I

ice cream 4, 22
Irish potato famine 42

K

kingdoms of life 4, 9

L

Leeuwenhoek, Anton van 5, 6, 18, 19

M

malaria 11, 15, 33, 34
microscopes 19
mitochondria 12, 13
mosquitoes 33, 34

N

nagana 35

O

orders (in classification) 9
organelles 12, 13

P

paramecia 11, 12, 14, 15, 30, 31

parasitic protists 15, 19, 29, 32, 33, 34, 35, 42

Phaeophyta (phylum) 21

photosynthesis 6, 10, 12, 13, 14, 15, 20, 26, 28

phylum 9

Phytophthora infestans 42

plankton 6, 10, 11, 16, 24, 25, 26

plants 4, 5, 6, 8, 10, 11, 14, 36

plasmodia 33, 34

plasmodial slime 38

Plasmodium (genus) 33

Plasmopara viticola 43

plastids 12, 13

potato blight 42

prokaryotic organisms 6

protists 4, 5, 6, 7, 8, 9, 12

animals (comparisons to) 4, 6, 8, 12

animals (protists living in) 7, 29, 30, 32, 33

carbon dioxide (protists and) 11, 14

cell structure 6, 8, 12, 13

cosmetics (use in) 11, 22

disease (causing of) 10, 11, 15, 33, 34, 35

feeding 6, 10, 11, 12, 14, 15, 28, 33, 36

food (for animals) 6, 10, 11, 16, 22, 26, 28

food (for humans) 6, 10, 11, 16, 22

habitats 7, 20, 29, 30, 36

humans (protists living in) 7, 15, 29, 30, 32 35

medicine (use in) 11, 22

movement 9, 12, 15, 24, 30, 31, 35, 38, 40

numbers of 10

oxygen (protists and) 11, 12, 14, 20

plants (comparisons to) 12, 13, 20

reproduction 19, 21, 25, 28, 37, 38

research (use in) 11, 37

protozoa 9, 15, 19, 29, 30, 31, 32, 33, 34, 35

pseudoplasmodia 40

pseudopodia 9, 15, 26, 29, 33

R

radiolaria 26

red blood cells 33, 34

red tide 11, 25

Rhodophyta (phylum) 21

rotifers 28

S

Sargasso Sea 23

Sargassum seaweed 23

seaweed 4, 8, 22, 23

sewage treatment 31

sharks 10, 11

slime molds 8, 36, 37, 38, 39

slime nets 40

species 9

Spirogyra 20, 21

sporangia 38, 41

sporozoans 12, 15, 29, 33

Stentor 31

sushi 22

T

Tokophrya 30

Trichia decipiens 38

Trypanosoma brucei 34

trypanosomes 34, 35

tsetse fly 35

V

Volvox 28

W

water molds 42

whales 10, 11, 16

white blood cells 34

White Cliffs of Dover, The, United Kingdom 17

World Health Organization (WHO) 33, 35

X

Xanthophyta (phylum) 21

Z

zygospores 21

ABOUT THE AUTHOR

Rona Arato has been a writer and editor for over 30 years. She has written for newspapers, magazines, Web sites, and corporate and not-for-profit organizations. In 2004, Rona began writing children's books. Her published books include *Fossils: Clues to Ancient Life* and *World of Water: Essential to life* for Crabtree Publishing. She has also written *Working for Freedom: The Story of Josiah Henson, Courage and Compassion, On a Canadian Day*, and *Mrs. Kaputnik's Pool Hall and Matzo Ball Emporium*.